The JAZZ PIANO CHORD BOOK

Published by
WISE PUBLICATIONS
14-15 Berners Street, London W1T 3LJ, UK.

Exclusive Distributors:

Contact us:
Hal Leonard
7777 West Bluemound Road
Milwaukee, WI 53213
Email: info@halleonard.com

In Europe, contact:
Hal Leonard Europe Limited
42 Wigmore Street
Marylebone, London, W1U 2RN
Email: info@halleonardeurope.com

In Australia, contact:
Hal Leonard Australia Pty. Ltd.
4 Lentara Court
Cheltenham, Victoria, 3192 Australia
Email: info@halleonard.com.au

Order No. AM1010196
ISBN 978-1-78305-865-5

Book devised and designed by Christopher Hussey.
Edited by Sam Lung.
Music engraved by Camden Music Services.
Cover designed by Michael Bell Design.

Your guarantee of quality:
As publishers, we strive to produce every book to
the highest commercial standards.
This book has been carefully designed to minimise awkward
page turns and to make playing from it a real pleasure.
Particular care has been given to specifying acid-free, neutral-sized paper
made from pulps which have not been elemental chlorine bleached.
This pulp is from farmed sustainable forests and was
produced with special regard for the environment.
Throughout, the printing and binding have been planned to ensure
a sturdy, attractive publication which should give years of enjoyment.
If your copy fails to meet our high standards,
please inform us and we will gladly replace it.

Introduction 4

How To Use This Book 6

Introduction

Jazz harmony is a defining feature of the style. Its extended chords, distinctive voicings and substitutions offer a wealth of opportunity for the pianist in particular. This book is designed to help piano players explore the possibilities of jazz harmony, with useful suggestions for voicing chords in an easy-to-use format.

The basic **triad** consists of the **1st**, **3rd** and **5th** degrees of the scale, whether it's major or minor, or the diminished or augmented variants of these chords.

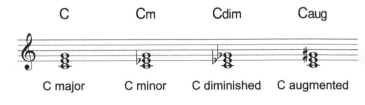

Jazz chords are often decorated by using the 7th and **extensions** above the 7th, i.e. the 9th, 11th and 13th. These extensions give chords a rich harmonic sound.

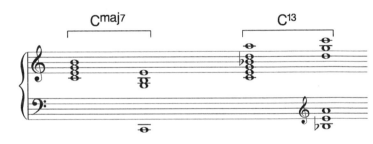

When you consider that the 5th, 9th, 11th and 13th can also be **altered** by putting an accidental (a flat ♭ or a sharp ♯) before it then you can see that there are many permutations that produce many different chords.

(Note: Strictly speaking, the 11th is never flattened and the 13th is never sharpened.)

For each chord there are many **voicings**—or different ways of playing the chord.

The voicing is affected by the order in which the notes of the chord are stacked. A number of voicing types have arisen through habit, theory and experiementation, such as **close position** and **open position**. With more elaborate chords a musician may also choose to omit certain notes—perhaps a bassist is playing the root anyway, or perhaps it just sounds 'right'.

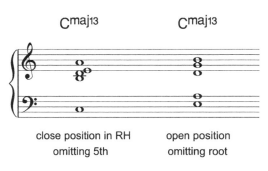

close position in RH   open position
omitting 5th   omitting root

There is almost no limit to the number of ways to voice a chord, and there is certainly no single definitive voicing for any one chord, however some voicings are more familiar to experienced jazz pianists.

This book does not attempt to be comprehensive, instead providing a guide to the most common chords and some of the more elaborate varieties through a selection of idiomatic voicings found throughout jazz, time and time again. For example, the piano riff underpinning the Miles Davis standard 'So What' can be formed from the Em[11] voicing on page 59 followed by the Dm[11] voicing on page 35, just as Bill Evans played it.

Enjoy exploring the different chord shapes and voicings in this book. A good harmonic understanding will enhance your musical appreciation and help to improve your playing, whether you are improvising a solo or realising the chords from a lead sheet. As you encounter new chords, try out the voicings provided and then experiment by creating your own voicings. You may find new ways of playing!

This book comprises 12 sections, each devoted to chords based on a common root. In order of appearance, the roots are: C, D♭, D, E♭, E, F, F♯, G, A♭, A, B♭ and B. You can thumb through to a different root using the labels at the edge of the pages.

For each root, the chords are grouped into families—*major, minor, suspended, augmented, dominant, diminished* and *slash chords*. These families are described in the header at the very top of each page, e.g. D suspended.

The box under each header shows the chords featuring on that page, in root position with all the notes of the chord stacked in order (i.e. root, 3rd, 5th, 7th, etc.). Here you can find out which notes are in any particular chord. Alternative names for these chords are also listed in this box (e.g. Caug *or:* C⁺).

The rest of the page is devoted to examples of two-handed voicings of these chords. To the right of the first example of each chord type there is also the option for a left-hand-only voicing— useful if you are playing a single melody line or solo in the right hand.

The '*See also*' section (at the bottom of some pages) lists related chords which can be found within this book—you could try some of these alternative chords as **substitutions** in certain situations.

Finding a chord

Let's say you want to find out how to play an E♭⁹ chord…

First, thumb through to the section devoted to chords with an E♭ root (beginning on page 44). As E♭⁹ is a **dominant** chord you should then use the headers to flick through to the 'E♭ dominant' section (pages 50–53). The boxes at the top will show which page features the E♭⁹ chord (for this example, page 50).

As well as the unopened 'stacked' voicing in the box (showing you the notes that are in the chord), you'll find two two-handed voicings of E♭⁹ on this page, as well as a left-hand-only voicing.

You can try the related chords (listed at the bottom) as substitutions, however they may not *always* work—for example, chords with an altered 9th (e.g. E♭¹³♭⁹♯¹¹) may clash with the melody—use your ear to judge.

Enharmonic variations

Enharmonic spellings are different ways of naming the same note. There are common enharmonic equivalents, like A♭ and G♯, and less common ones, like B and C♭, or A and B♭♭!

In sections where the root can be expressed as a flat (♭) or a sharp (♯), the more common enharmonic spelling has been employed, for example D♭ rather than C♯. So, if you need to find a C♯ᵐᵃʲ⁷ chord then look in the D♭ section— D♭ᵐᵃʲ⁷ is the same chord, spelt differently.

For some pages in these sections, the alternative spelling is used where it is more usual to see a family of chords named in this way and where it makes the chords easier to read, for example the C♯ minor chords (in the D♭ section, pages 22–23).

There is also some variation in the enharmonic spelling of individual notes in some chords. In the boxes at the top of each page, the chords are spelt accurately according to how the notes are named in the key—this sometimes involves double flats ♭♭ or double sharps x and often a large number of accidentals in certain keys! However, in the voicings that follow on these pages, certain notes have been enharmonically respelt to make the voicings easier to read.

C

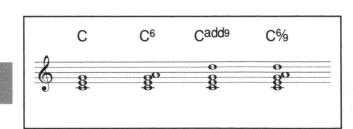

C6

C6

Cadd9

C6/9

C6/9

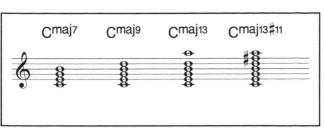

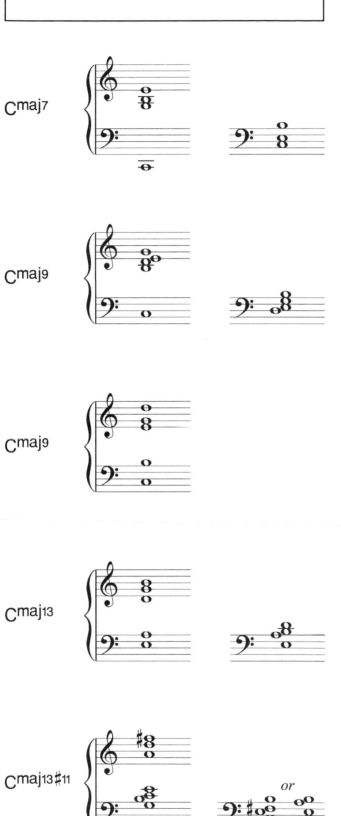

See also: C^{maj7♯5}

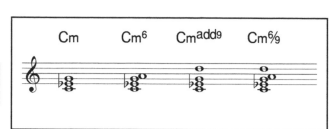

C

Cm⁶

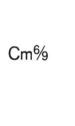

Cm^add9

Cm⁶⁄₉

Cm⁶⁄₉

Cm⁶⁄₉

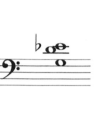

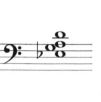

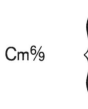

C minor

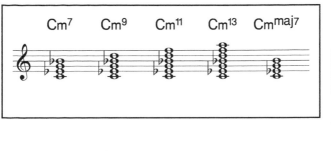

Cm⁷   Cm⁹   Cm¹¹   Cm¹³   Cmᵐᵃʲ⁷

C

Cm⁷

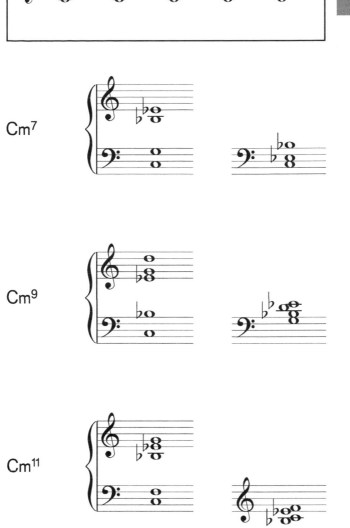

Cm⁹

Cm¹¹

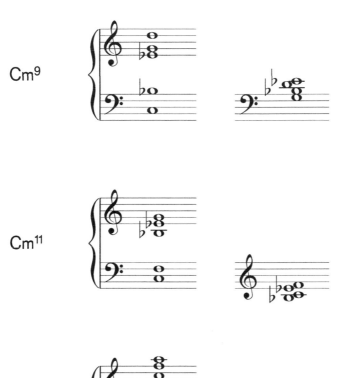

Cm¹³

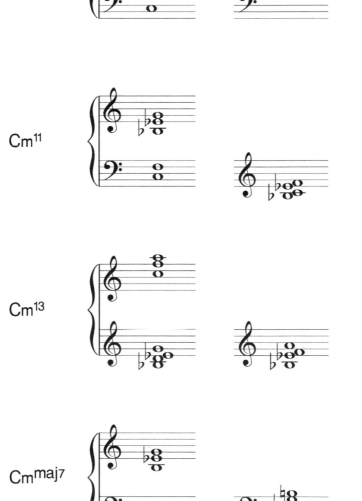

Cmᵐᵃʲ⁷

See also: Cm⁷♭⁵ *(or C∅)*

11

C

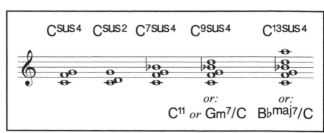

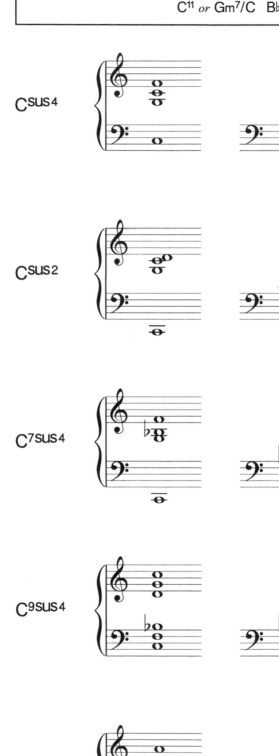

See also: C7sus4♭9, C13sus4♭9, B♭/C, Gm7/C, B♭maj7/C

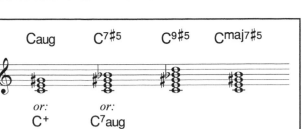

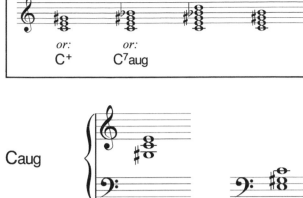

Caug

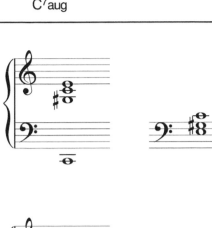

C⁷♯5

C⁷♯5

C⁹♯5

Cmaj7♯5

See also: C⁷♭9♭13, C⁷♯9♭13

C

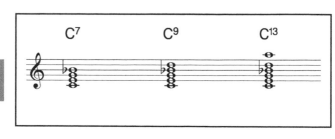

C⁷

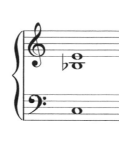 

C⁹

 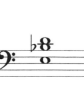

C⁹

 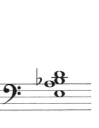

C¹³

C¹³

See also: C⁷ˢᵘˢ⁴, C⁷♭⁵, C⁷♯⁵, C⁷♭⁹, C⁷♯⁹, C⁷ˢᵘˢ⁴♭⁹, C⁷♭⁹♭¹³, C⁷♯⁹♭¹³, C⁹♯¹¹, C¹³♭⁹♯¹¹, B♭/C, Gm⁷/C, B♭ᵐᵃʲ⁷/C, F♯/C, A/C (and any extended variants of these chords)

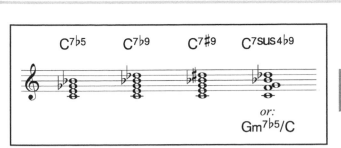

C

$C^{7\flat5}$

$C^{7\flat9}$

$C^{7\flat9}$

$C^{7\sharp9}$

$C^{7sus4\flat9}$

C

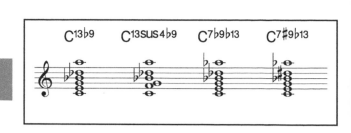

$C^{13\flat9}$

$C^{13sus4\flat9}$

$C^{7\flat9\flat13}$

$C^{7\sharp9\flat13}$

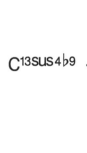 

$C^{7\sharp9\flat13}$

See also: A/C

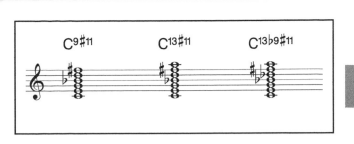

C

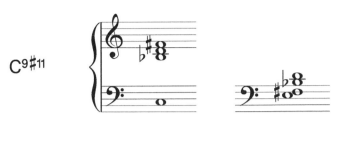

C⁹♯¹¹

C⁹♯¹¹

C¹³♯¹¹

C¹³♯¹¹

C¹³♭9♯¹¹

See also: F♯/C

C

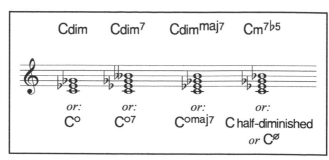

Cdim   Cdim⁷   Cdim^maj7   Cm⁷♭⁵

or: *or:*   *or:*   *or:*
C°   C°⁷   C°maj7   C half-diminished
                                    or C^ø

Cdim

Cdim⁷

Cdim^maj7

Cm⁷♭⁵

Cm⁷♭⁵

C

Bb/C

or:

C¹¹

or

C⁹sus4

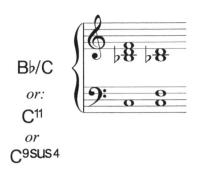

Gm⁷/C

or:

C¹¹

or

C⁹sus4

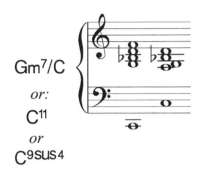

Bbmaj7/C

or:

C¹³sus4

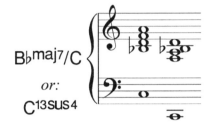

F#/C

or:

C⁷b9#11

or

C⁷b5b9

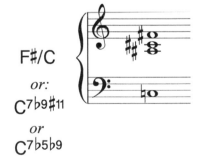

A/C

or:

C¹³b9

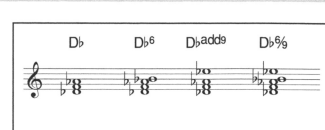

Db   Db⁶   Dbadd⁹   Db⁶⁄₉

D♭

D♭⁶

D♭⁶

D♭add⁹

D♭⁶⁄₉

D♭⁶⁄₉

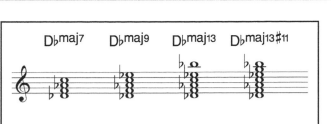

D♭

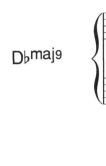

D♭maj7

D♭maj9

D♭maj9

D♭maj13

D♭maj13♯11

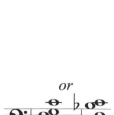

or

See also: D♭maj7♯5

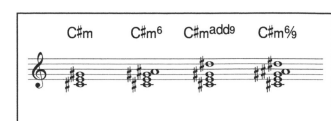

Db

C#m⁶

C#m^add9

C#m⁶⁄₉

C#m⁶⁄₉

C#m⁶⁄₉

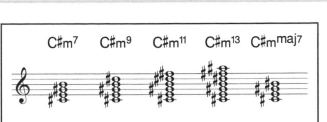

**D♭**

C♯m⁷

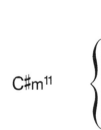

C♯m⁹

C♯m¹¹

C♯m¹³

C♯mᵐᵃʲ⁷

See also: C♯m⁷♭⁵ (or C♯ø)

D♭ suspended

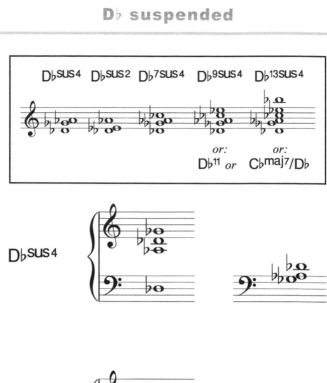

Db^{sus4}   Db^{sus2}   Db^{7sus4}   Db^{9sus4}   Db^{13sus4}

or:
Db¹¹ or   Cb^{maj7}/Db

Db

D♭ sus4

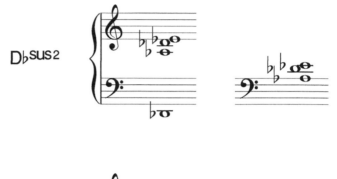

D♭ sus2

D♭ 7sus4

D♭ 9sus4

D♭ 13sus4

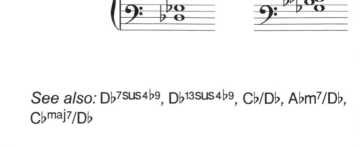

See also: Db^{7sus4♭9}, Db^{13sus4♭9}, Cb/Db, Abm⁷/Db, Cb^{maj7}/Db

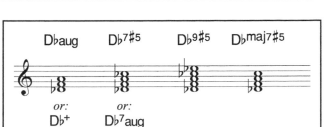

Db

D♭aug

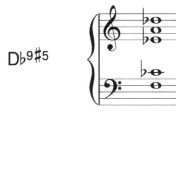

D♭7♯5

D♭7♯5

D♭9♯5

D♭maj7♯5

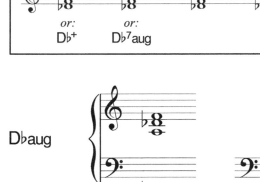

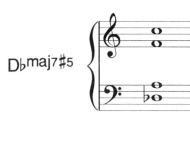

See also: D♭7♭9♭13, D♭7♯9♭13

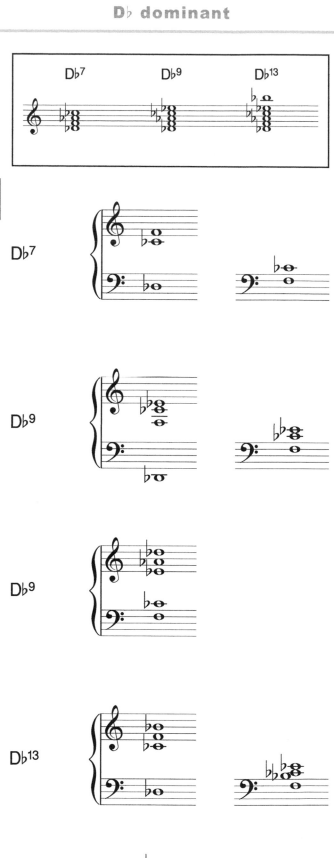

D♭

D♭7

D♭9

D♭9

D♭13

D♭13

See also: D♭7sus4, D♭7♭5, D♭7♯5, D♭7♭9, D♭7♯9, D♭7sus4♭9, D♭7♭9♭13, D♭7♯9♭13, D♭9♯11, D♭13♭9♯11, C♭/D♭, A♭m7/D♭, C♭maj7/D♭, G/D♭, B♭/D♭ (and any extended variants of these chords)

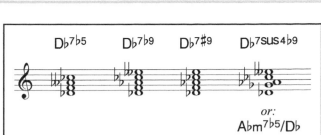
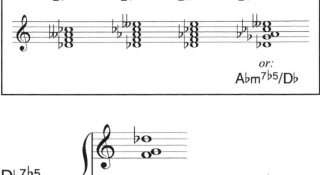

Db7b5   Db7b9   Db7#9   Db7sus4b9

or:
A♭m7b5/Db

D♭

Db7b5

Db7b9

Db7b9
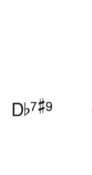

Db7#9

Db7sus4b9

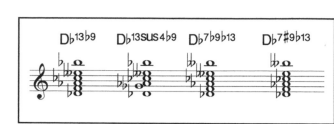

D♭

D♭13♭9

D♭13sus4♭9

D♭7♭9♭13

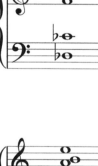

D♭7♯9♭13

D♭7♯9♭13

See also: B♭/D♭

D♭ dominant

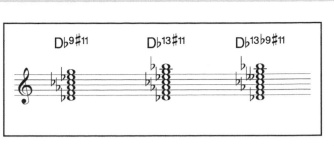

D♭9#11

D♭9#11

D♭9#11

D♭13#11

D♭13#11

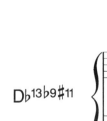

D♭13♭9#11

See also: G/D♭

29

D♭

C#dim

C#dim⁷

C#dim^maj7

C#m⁷♭⁵

C#m⁷♭⁵

D♭

B/C♯
or:
C♯11
or
C♯9sus4

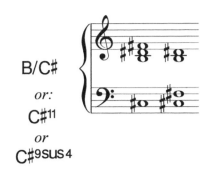

A♭m7/D♭
or:
D♭11
or
D♭9sus4

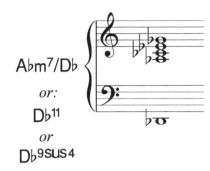

Bmaj7/C♯
or:
C♯13sus4

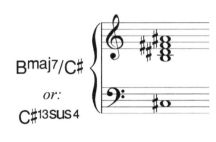

G/D♭
or:
D♭7♭9♯11
or
D♭7♭5♭9

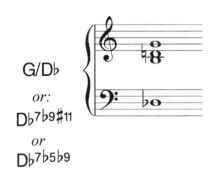

B♭/D♭
or:
D♭13♭9

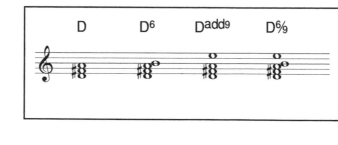

D   D⁶   Dadd9   D⁶⁄₉

D

D⁶

D⁶

Dadd9

D⁶⁄₉

D⁶⁄₉

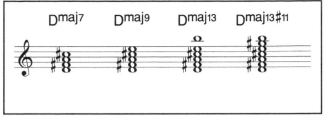

Dmaj7

Dmaj9

Dmaj9

Dmaj13

Dmaj13#11

or

See also: D^{maj7#5}

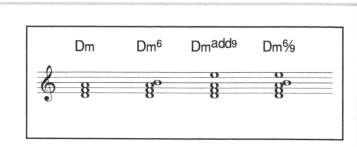

Dm   Dm⁶   Dmᵃᵈᵈ⁹   Dm⁶⁄₉

D

Dm⁶

Dmᵃᵈᵈ⁹

Dm⁶⁄₉

Dm⁶⁄₉

Dm⁶⁄₉

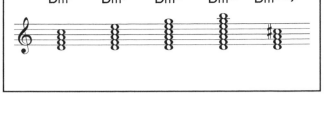

Dm⁷

D

Dm⁹

Dm¹¹

Dm¹³

Dmᵐᵃʲ⁷

See also: Dm⁷♭⁵ *(or* D⌀*)*

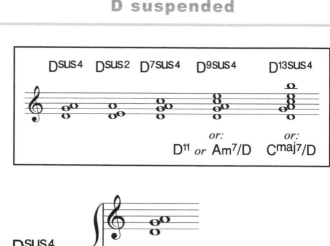

D

D^{sus4}

D^{sus2}

D^{7sus4}

D^{9sus4}

D^{13sus4}

See also: D^{7sus4♭9}, D^{13sus4♭9}, C/D, Am⁷/D, C^{maj7}/D

D augmented

Daug   D7♯5   D9♯5   Dmaj7♯5

or: or:
D+   D7aug

Daug

D7♯5

D7♯5

D9♯5

Dmaj7♯5

See also: D7♭9♭13, D7♯9♭13

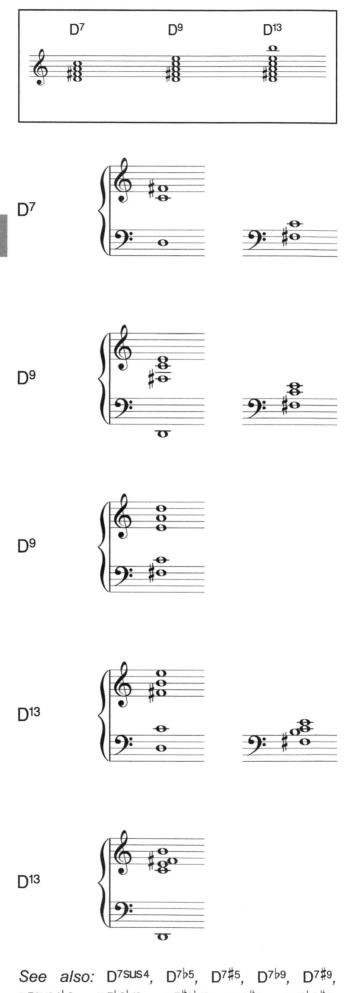

D⁷   D⁹   D¹³

D⁷

D⁹

D⁹

D¹³

D¹³

See also: D⁷ˢᵘˢ⁴, D⁷♭⁵, D⁷♯⁵, D⁷♭⁹, D⁷♯⁹, D⁷ˢᵘˢ⁴♭⁹, D⁷♭⁹♭¹³, D⁷♯⁹♭¹³, D⁹♯¹¹, D¹³♭⁹♯¹¹, C/D, Am⁷/D, Cᵐᵃʲ⁷/D, A♭/D, B/D (and any extended variants of these chords)

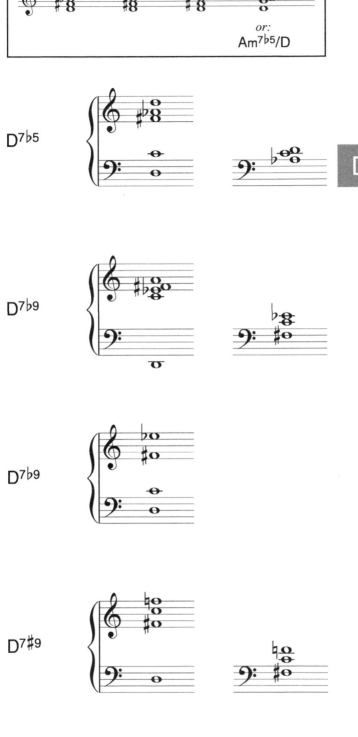

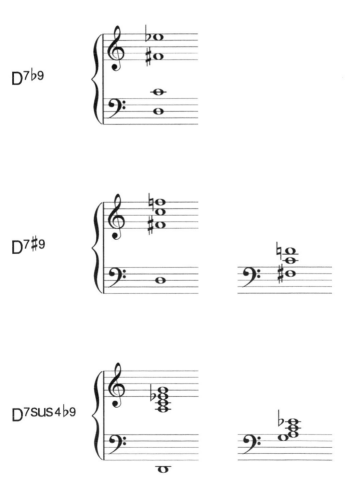

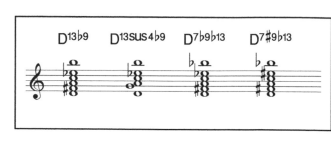

D

D¹³♭9

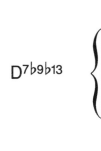

D¹³sus4♭9

D⁷♭9♭13

D⁷♯9♭13

D⁷♯9♭13

See also: B/D

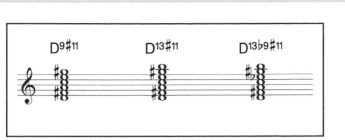

D⁹♯11

D⁹♯11

D¹³♯11

D¹³♯11

D¹³♭9♯11

D

See also: A♭/D

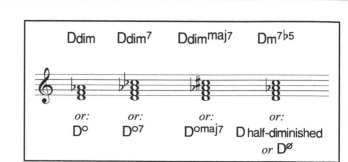

D

Ddim

Ddim⁷

Ddim^maj7

Dm⁷♭5

Dm⁷♭5

C/D

or:
D¹¹

or
D⁹sus4

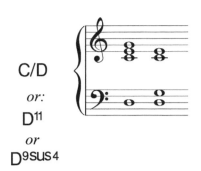

D

Am⁷/D

or:
D¹¹

or
D⁹sus4

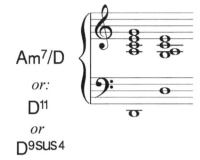

C^{maj7}/D

or:
D¹³sus4

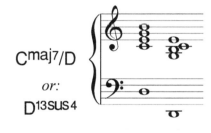

A♭/D

or:
D^{7♭9♯11}

or
D^{7♭5♭9}

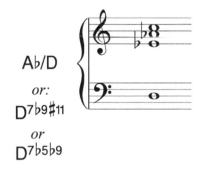

B/D

or:
D^{13♭9}

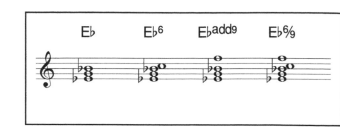

E♭ 6

E♭ 6

E♭ add9

E♭ 6/9

E♭ 6/9

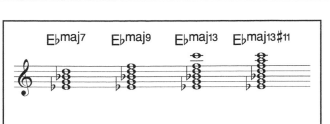

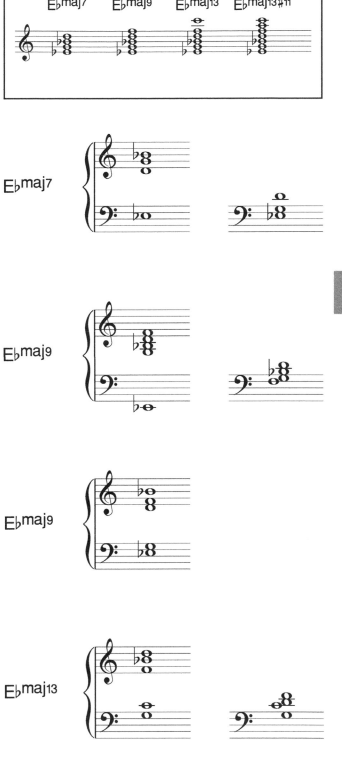

E♭

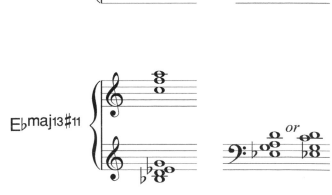

See also: E♭maj7♯5

Ebm⁶

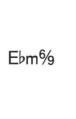

Ebm^add9

Ebm⁶⁄₉

Ebm⁶⁄₉

Ebm⁶⁄₉

E♭m⁷

E♭m⁹

E♭m¹¹

E♭m¹³

E♭mᵐᵃʲ⁷

See also: E♭m⁷♭⁵ *(or* E♭ø*)*

E♭ suspended

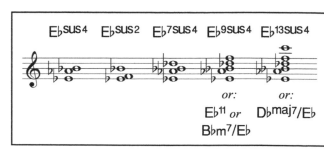

E♭SUS4   E♭SUS2   E♭7SUS4   E♭9SUS4   E♭13SUS4

or: *or:*
E♭11 *or*   D♭maj7/E♭
B♭m7/E♭

E♭

E♭SUS4

E♭SUS2

E♭7SUS4

E♭9SUS4

E♭13SUS4

See also: E♭7SUS4♭9, E♭13SUS4♭9, D♭/E♭, B♭m7/E♭, D♭maj7/E♭

Eb augmented

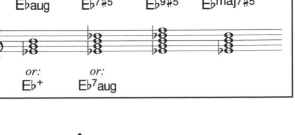

Ebaug
or:
Eb+

Eb7#5
or:
Eb7aug

Eb9#5

Ebmaj7#5

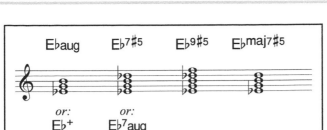

Ebaug

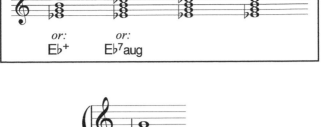

Eb7#5

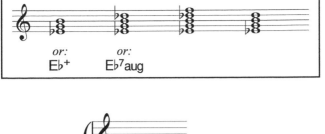

Eb7#5

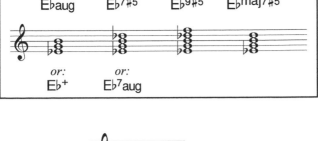

Eb9#5

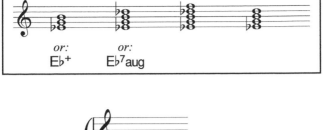

Ebmaj7#5

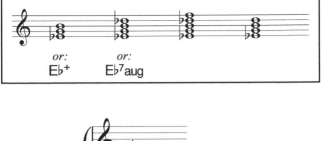

See also: Eb7b9b13, Eb7#9b13

Eb

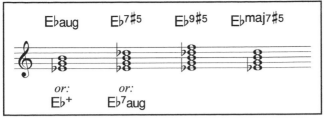

49

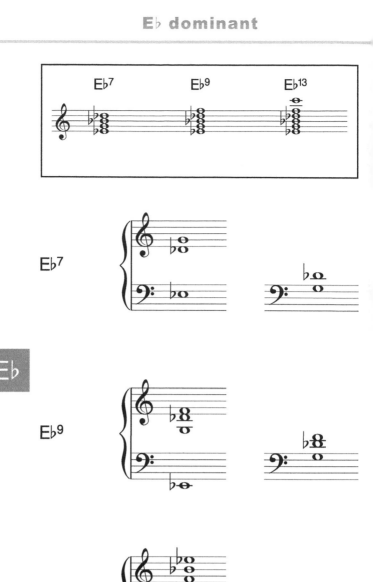

E♭

E♭7

E♭9

E♭9

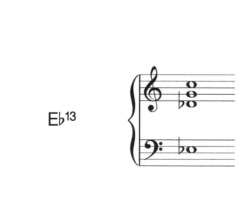

E♭13

E♭13

See also: E♭7sus4, E♭7♭5, E♭7♯5, E♭7♭9, E♭7♯9, E♭7sus4♭9, E♭7♭9♭13, E♭7♯9♭13, E♭9♯11, E♭13♭9♯11, D♭/E♭, B♭m7/E♭, D♭maj7/E♭, A/E♭, C/E♭ (and any extended variants of these chords)

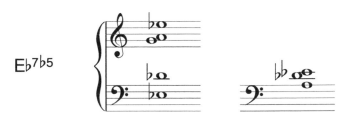

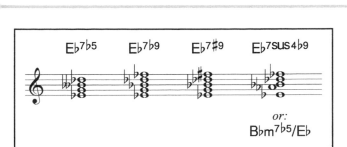

or:
B♭m⁷♭⁵/E♭

E♭⁷♭⁵

E♭

E♭⁷♭⁹

E♭⁷♭⁹

E♭⁷♯⁹

E♭⁷sus4♭⁹

E♭^{13♭9}

E♭

E♭^{13sus4♭9}

E♭^{7♭9♭13}

E♭^{7♯9♭13}

E♭^{7♯9♭13}

See also: C/E♭

Eb dominant

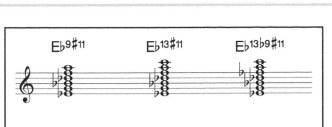

Eb9#11

Eb9#11

Eb13#11

Eb13#11

Eb13b9#11

See also: A/Eb

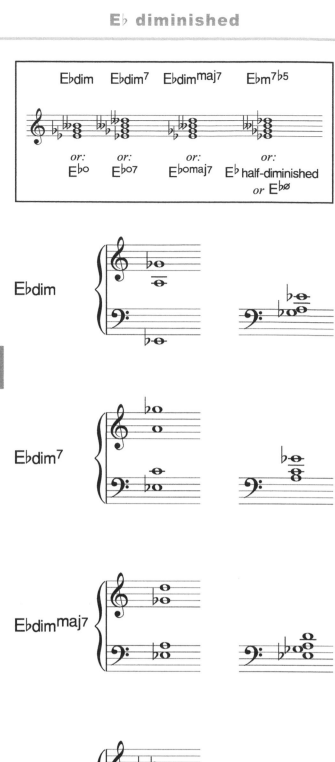

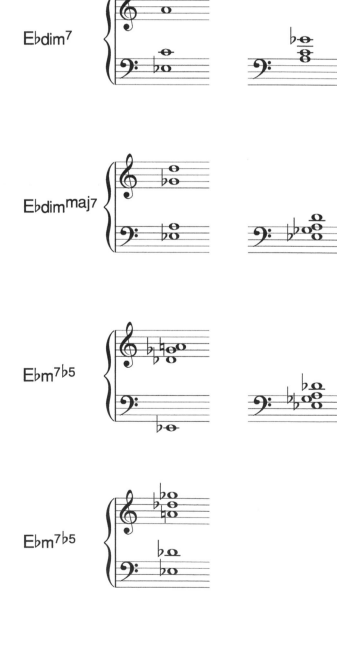

Db/Eb
or:
Eb11
or
Eb9sus4

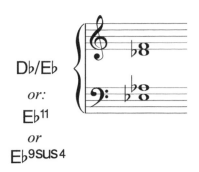

Bbm7/Eb
or:
Eb11
or
Eb9sus4

Eb

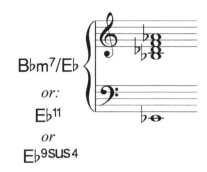

Dbmaj7/Eb
or:
Eb13sus4

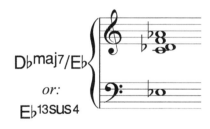

A/Eb
or:
Eb7b9#11
or
Eb7b5b9

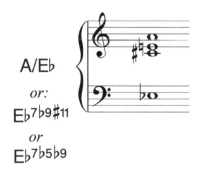

C/Eb
or:
Eb13b9

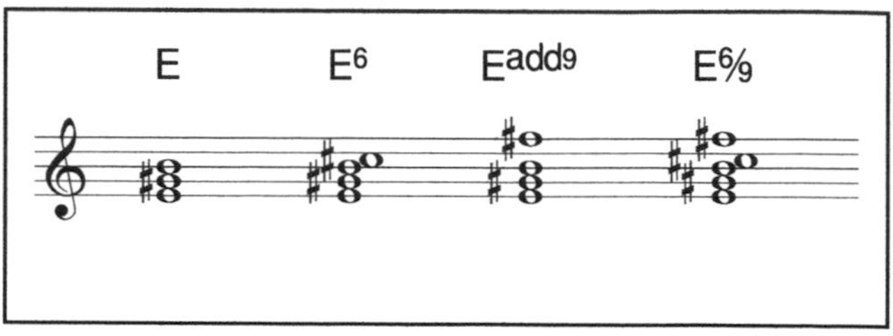

E⁶

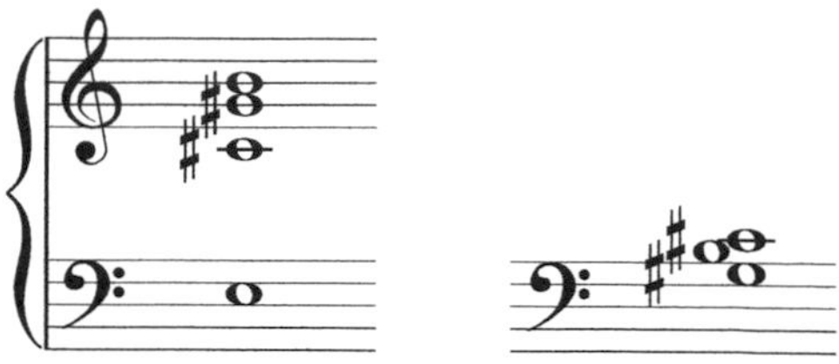

E

E⁶

Eadd9

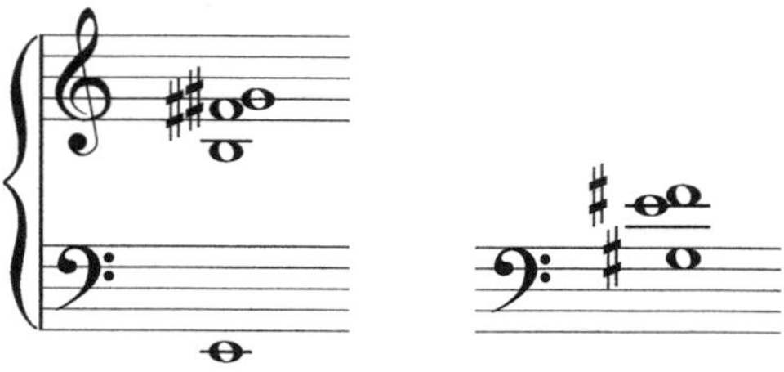

E⁶⁄₉

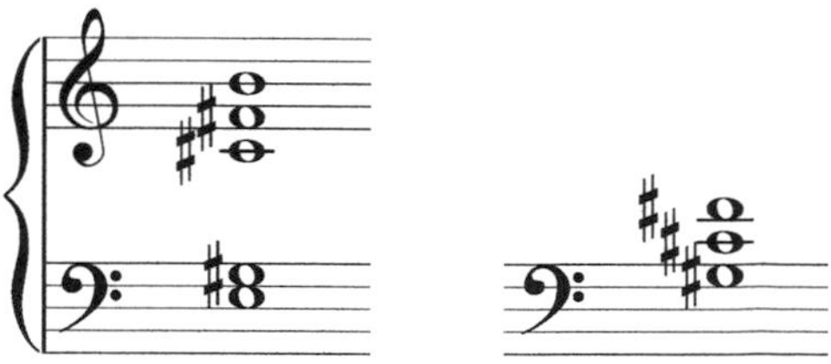

E⁶⁄₉

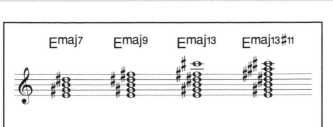

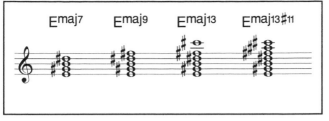

Emaj7

Emaj9

E

Emaj9

Emaj13

Emaj13♯11

See also: E^{maj7}♯5

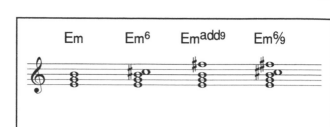

Em **Em⁶** **Em^add9** **Em⁶/₉**

Em⁶

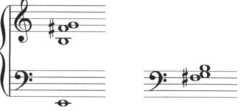

Em^add9

E

Em⁶/₉

Em⁶/₉

Em⁶/₉

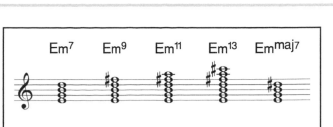

Em⁷

Em⁹

E

Em¹¹

Em¹³

Em^maj7

See also: Em⁷♭5 *(or* E^ø *)*

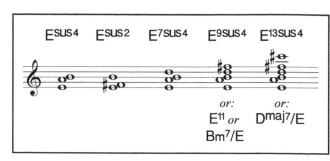

E^{SUS4} E^{SUS2} E^{7SUS4} E^{9SUS4} E^{13SUS4}

or: *or:*
E¹¹ *or* D^{maj7}/E
Bm⁷/E

E^{SUS4}

E^{SUS2}

E^{7SUS4}

E^{9SUS4}

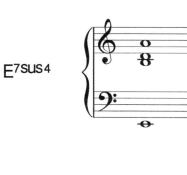

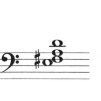

E^{13SUS4}

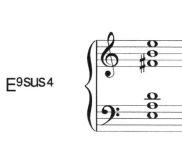

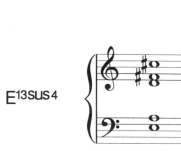

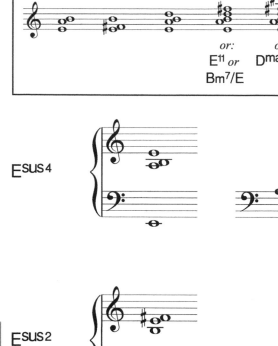

See also: E^{7SUS4♭9}, E^{13SUS4♭9}, D/E, Bm⁷/E, D^{maj7}/E

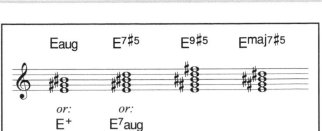

Eaug

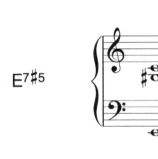

E7♯5

E7♯5

E9♯5

Emaj7♯5

See also: E7♭9♭13, E7♯9♭13

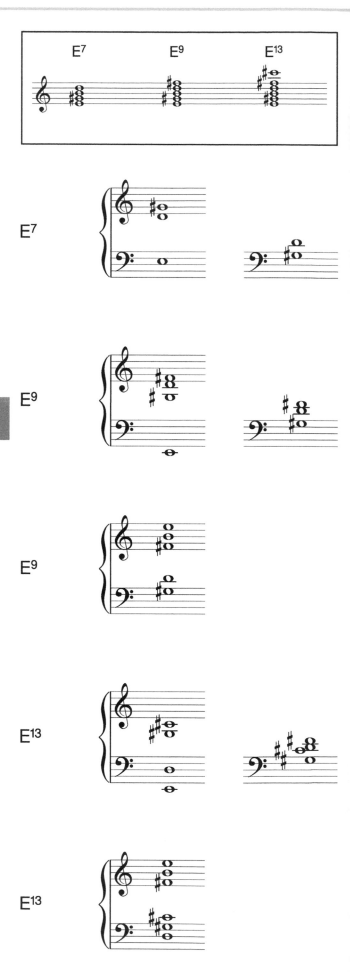

See also: E7sus4, E7♭5, E7♯5, E7♭9, E7♯9, E7sus4♭9, E7♭9♭13, E7♯9♭13, E9♯11, E13♭9♯11, D/E, Bm7/E, Dmaj7/E, B♭/E, C♯/E (and any extended variants of these chords)

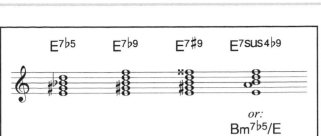

E7♭5

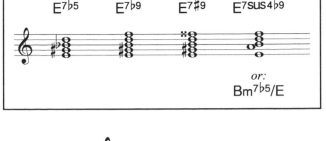

E7♭9

E

E7♭9

E7♯9

E7sus4♭9

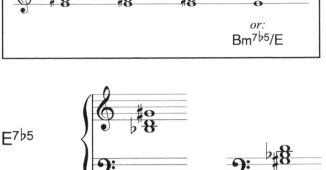

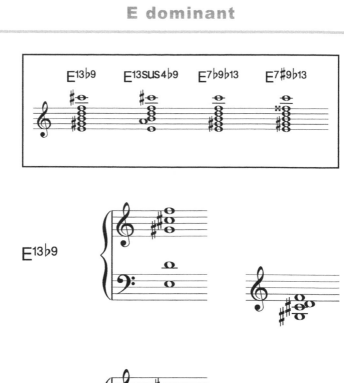

E13♭9

E13SUS4♭9

E7♭9♭13

E7♯9♭13

E7♯9♭13

See also: C♯/E

E9♯11

E9♯11

E

E13♯11

E13♯11

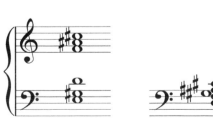

E13♭9♯11

See also: B♭/E

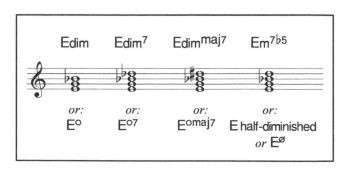

Edim

Edim⁷

Edim^maj7

Em⁷♭5

Em⁷♭5

D/E
or:
E¹¹
or
E⁹SUS4

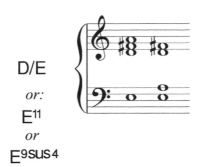

Bm⁷/E
or:
E¹¹
or
E⁹SUS4

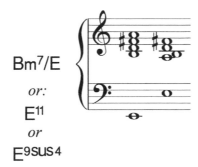

Dmaj7/E
or:
E¹³SUS4

E

Bb/E
or:
E⁷♭9♯11
or
E⁷♭5♭9

Db/E
or:
E¹³♭9

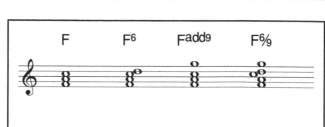

F major

F6

F6

Fadd9

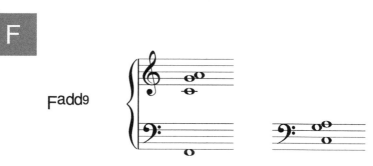

F6/9

F6/9

F major

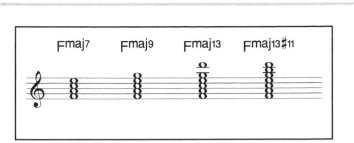

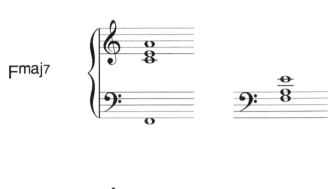

Fmaj7

Fmaj9

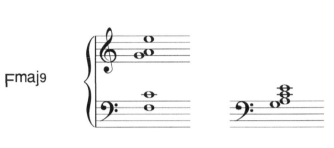

Fmaj9

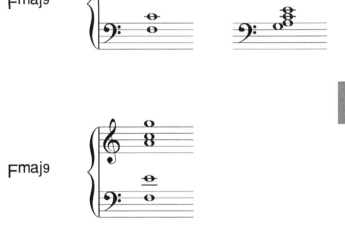

Fmaj13

Fmaj13#11

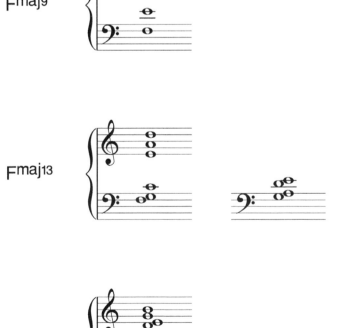

See also: F^maj7#5

F minor

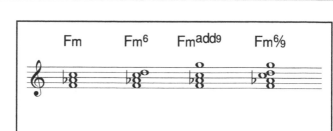

Fm⁶

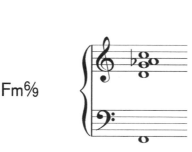

Fmadd9

Fm⁶⁄₉

Fm⁶⁄₉

Fm⁶⁄₉

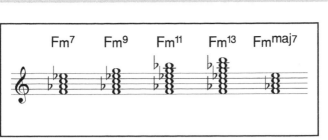

Fm⁷

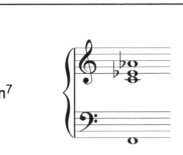

Fm⁹

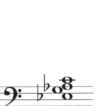

Fm¹¹

Fm¹³

Fmᵐᵃʲ⁷

See also: Fm⁷♭⁵ *(or* F∅*)*

F suspended

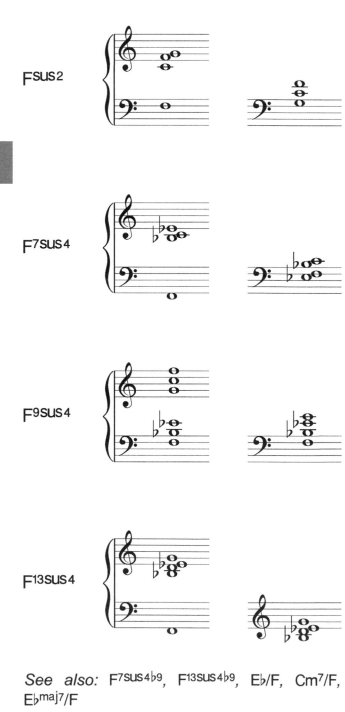

See also: F7sus4♭9, F13sus4♭9, E♭/F, Cm7/F, E♭maj7/F

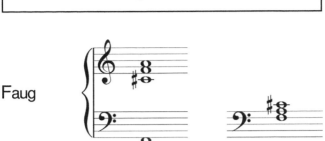

Faug

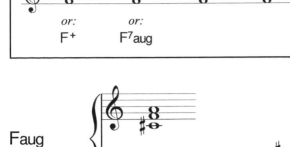

F7#5

F7#5

F9#5

Fmaj7#5

F

See also: F7♭9♭13, F7#9♭13

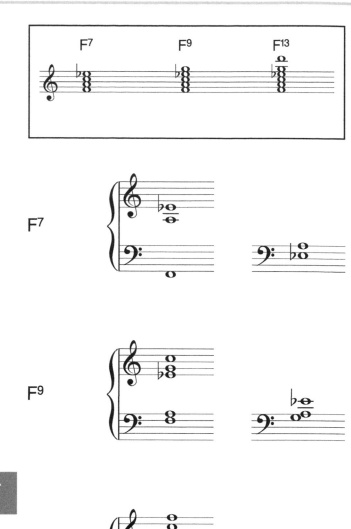

F7

F9

F

F9

F13

F13

See also: F7sus4, F7♭5, F7♯5, F7♭9, F7♯9, F7sus4♭9, F7♭9♭13, F7♯9♭13, F9♯11, F13♭9♯11, E♭/F, Cm7/F, E♭maj7/F, B/F, D/F (and any extended variants of these chords)

F⁷♭5

F⁷♭9

F⁷♭9

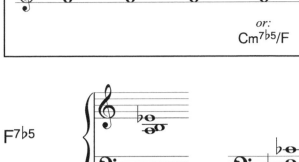

F⁷♯9

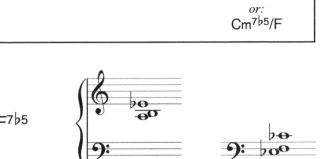

F⁷sus4♭9

F

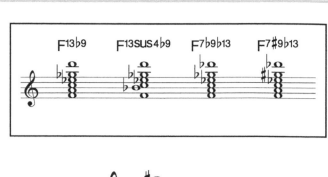

F13♭9

F13SUS4♭9

F7♭9♭13

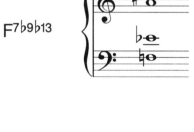

F7♯9♭13

F7♯9♭13

See also: D/F

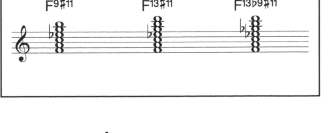

F9#11

F9#11

F13#11

F13#11

F13b9#11

F

See also: B/F

F diminished

Fdim

Fdim⁷

Fdim^maj7

Fm⁷♭5

Fm⁷♭5

Eb/F
or:
F¹¹
or
F⁹sus4

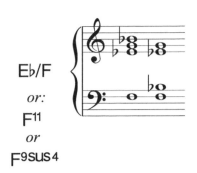

Cm⁷/F
or:
F¹¹
or
F⁹sus4

Ebmaj7/F
or:
F¹³sus4

B/F
or:
F⁷b9♯11
or
F⁷b5b9

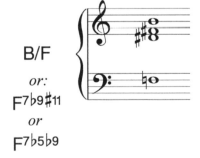

D/F
or:
F¹³b9

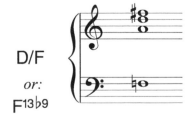

F

Gb6

Gb6

Gbadd9

Gb6/9

Gb6/9

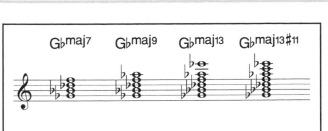

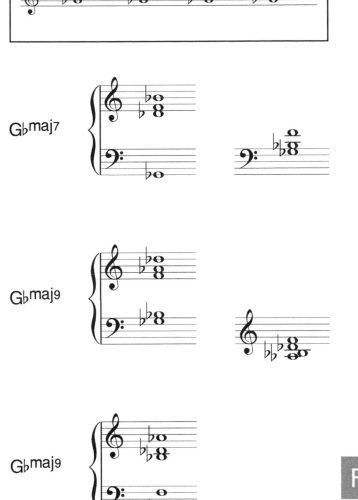

Gbmaj7

Gbmaj9

Gbmaj9

Gbmaj13

Gbmaj13♯11

See also: Gbmaj7♯5

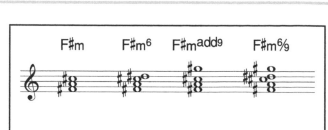

F♯m6

F♯madd9

F♯m6⁄9

F♯m6⁄9

F♯m6⁄9

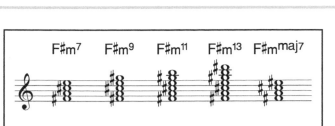

F♯m⁷

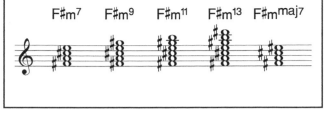

F♯m⁹

F♯m¹¹

F♯m¹³

F♯mᵐᵃʲ⁷

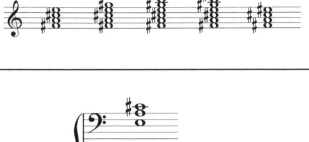

See also: F♯m⁷♭⁵ *(or* F♯∅*)*

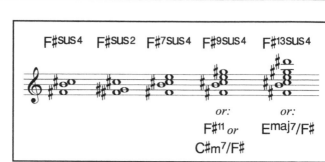

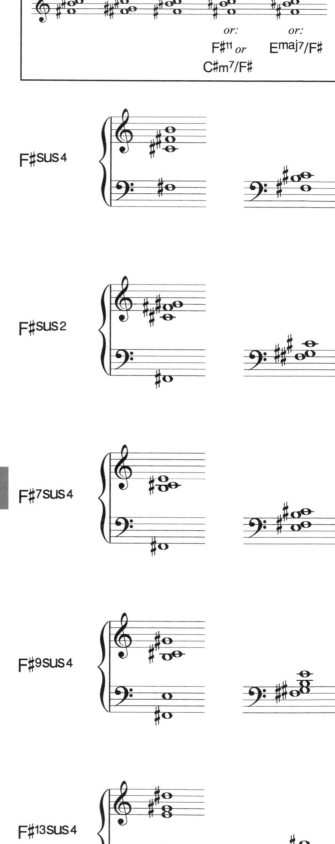

F♯SUS4

F♯SUS2

F♯

F♯7SUS4

F♯9SUS4

F♯13SUS4

See also: F♯7sus4♭9, F♯13sus4♭9, E/F♯, C♯m7/F♯, Emaj7/F♯

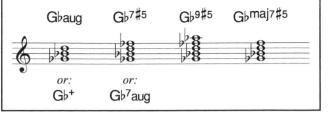

Gᵇaug

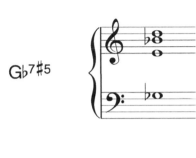

Gᵇ7♯5

Gᵇ7♯5

F♯

Gᵇ9♯5

Gᵇmaj7♯5

See also: F♯7♭9♭13, F♯7♯9♭13

See also: F♯7sus4, F♯7♭5, F♯7♯5, F♯7♭9, F♯7♯9, F♯7sus4♭9, F♯7♭9♭13, F♯7♯9♭13, F♯9♯11, F♯13♭9♯11, E/F♯, C♯m7/F♯, Emaj7/F♯, C/F♯, D♯/F♯ (and any extended variants of these chords)

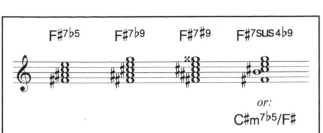

F♯7♭5   F♯7♭9   F♯7♯9   F♯7sus4♭9

or:
C♯m7♭5/F♯

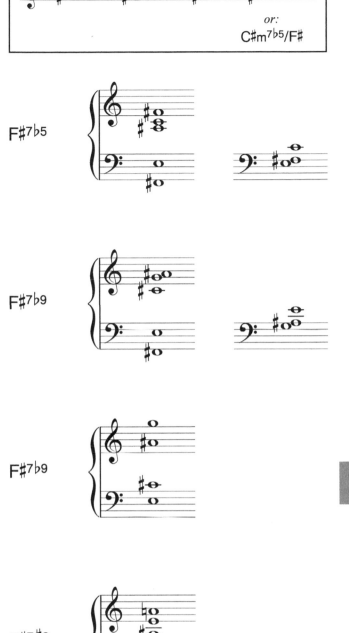

F♯7♭5

F♯7♭9

F♯7♭9

F♯

F♯7♯9

F♯7sus4♭9

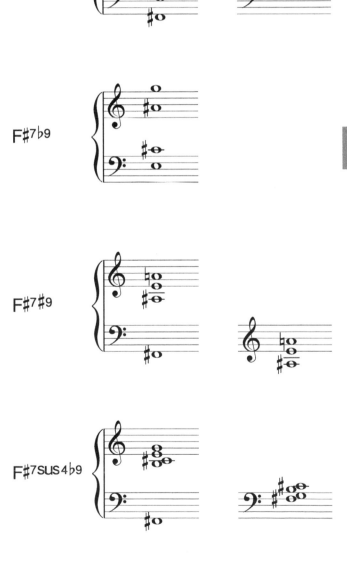

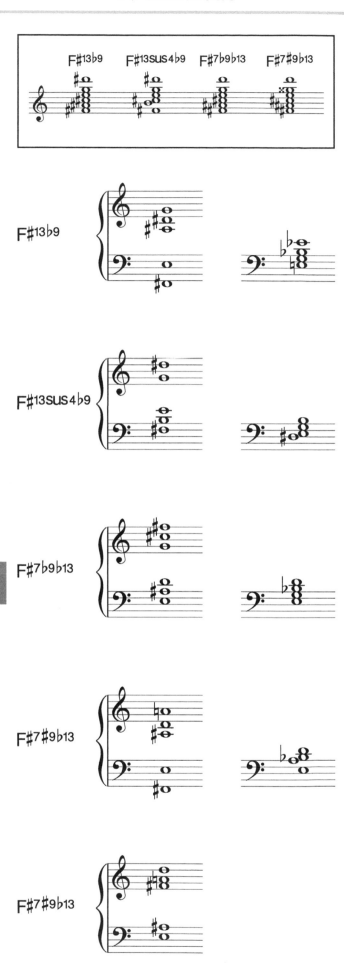

F♯13♭9

F♯13sus4♭9

F♯7♭9♭13

F♯7♯9♭13

F♯7♯9♭13

F♯

See also: D♯/F♯

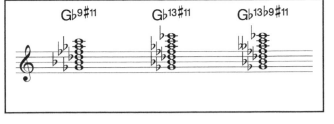

G♭9♯11

G♭9♯11

G♭13♯11

F♯

G♭13♯11

G♭13♭9♯11

See also: C/F♯

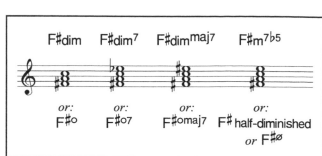

F#dim   F#dim⁷   F#dim^maj7   F#m⁷♭⁵

or: or: or: or:
F♯o   F♯o7   F♯omaj7   F♯ half-diminished
                                 or F♯ø

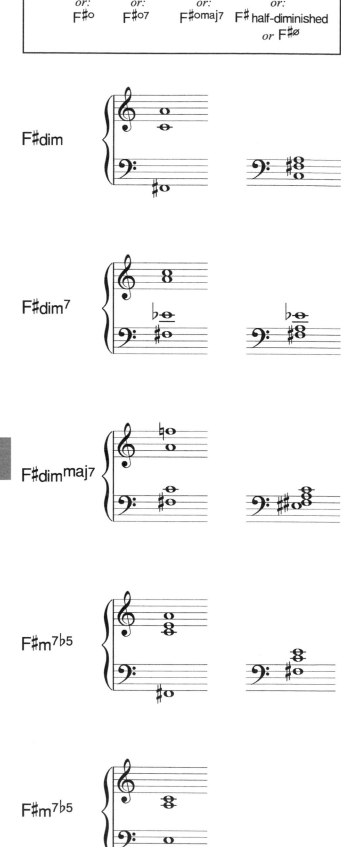

F#dim

F#dim⁷

F♯

F#dim^maj7

F#m⁷♭⁵

F#m⁷♭⁵

E/F♯

or:

F♯11

or

F♯9sus4

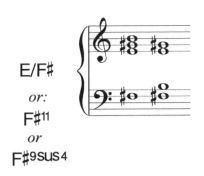

C♯m7/F♯

or:

F♯11

or

F♯9sus4

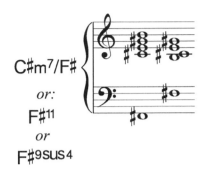

Emaj7/F♯

or:

F♯13sus4

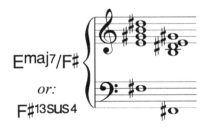

F♯

C/F♯

or:

F♯7b9♯11

or

F♯7b5b9

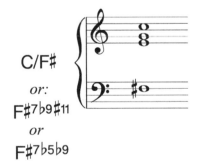

Eb/F♯

or:

F♯13b9

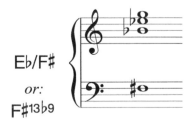

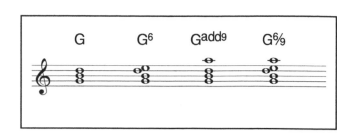

G   G⁶   Gadd9   G⁶⁄₉

G⁶

G⁶

Gadd9

G

G⁶⁄₉

G⁶⁄₉

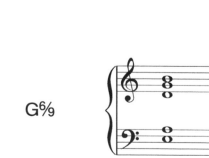

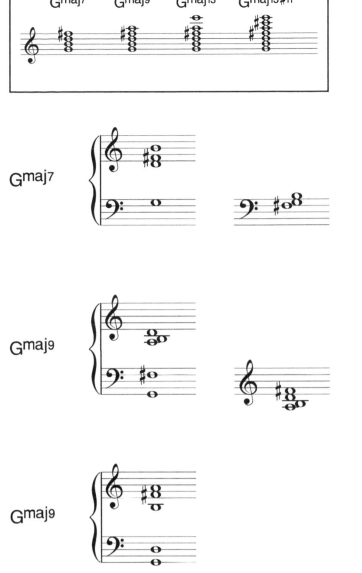

G

See also: Gmaj7♯5

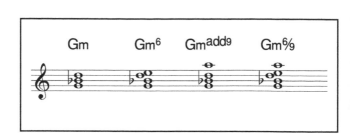

Gm   Gm⁶   Gmᵃᵈᵈ⁹   Gm⁶⁄₉

Gm⁶

Gmᵃᵈᵈ⁹

Gm⁶⁄₉

Gm⁶⁄₉

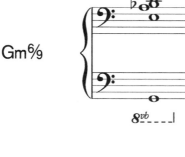

8vb

Gm⁶⁄₉

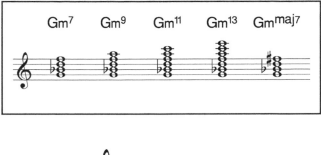

Gm7

Gm9

Gm11

G

Gm13

Gm^maj7

8vb

See also: Gm7♭5 *(or G∅)*

See also: G^{7sus4♭9}, G^{13sus4♭9}, F/G, Dm⁷/G, F^{maj7}/G

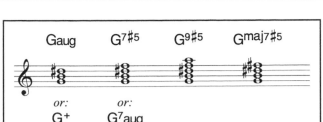
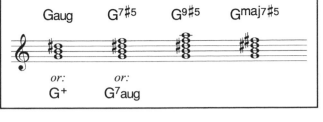

Gaug

G⁷♯⁵

G⁷♯⁵

G⁹♯⁵

G

Gᵐᵃʲ⁷♯⁵

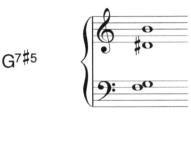

See also: G⁷♭⁹♭¹³, G⁷♯⁹♭¹³

See also: G7sus4, G7♭5, G7♯5, G7♭9, G7♯9, G7sus4♭9, G7♭9♭13, G7♯9♭13, G9♯11, G13♭9♯11, F/G, Dm7/G, Fmaj7/G, D♭/G, E/G (and any extended variants of these chords)

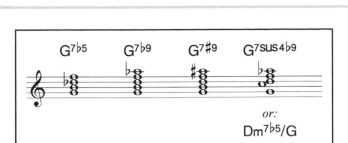

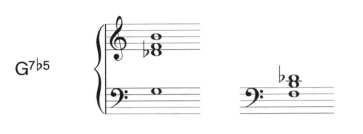

G7♭5

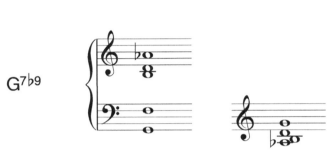

G7♭9

G7♭9

G7#9

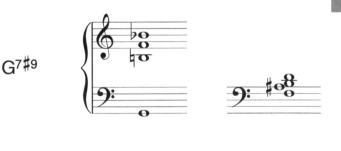

G7sus4♭9

G

See also: E/G

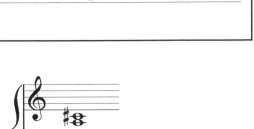

G⁹♯11

G⁹♯¹¹

G¹³♯¹¹

G¹³♯¹¹

G¹³♭⁹♯¹¹

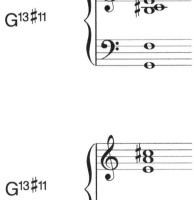

G

See also: D♭/G

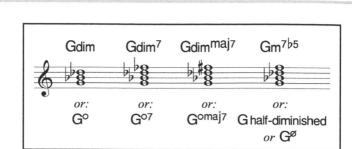

Gdim

Gdim⁷

Gdim^maj7

G

Gm⁷♭5

Gm⁷♭5

F/G
or:
G¹¹
or
G⁹sus4

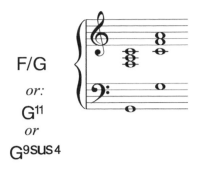

Dm⁷/G
or:
G¹¹
or
G⁹sus4

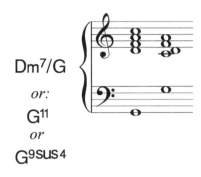

Fmaj7/G
or:
G¹³sus4

Db/G
or:
G⁷♭9♯11
or
G⁷♭5♭9

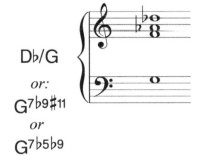

G

E/G
or:
G¹³♭9

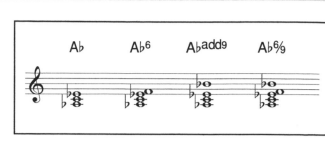

A♭   A♭6   A♭add9   A♭6/9

A♭6

A♭6

A♭add9

A♭   A♭6/9

A♭6/9

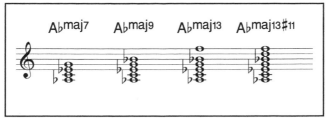

A♭maj7

A♭maj9

A♭maj9

A♭maj13

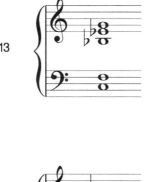

A♭maj13♯11

See also: A♭maj7♯5

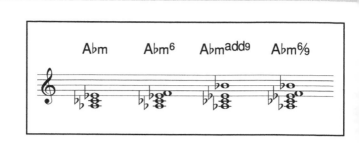

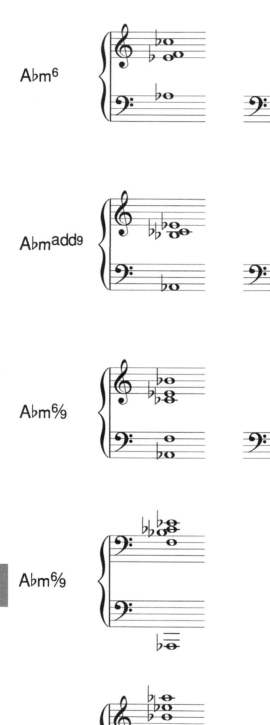

A♭m⁶

A♭madd9

A♭m6/9

A♭m6/9

A♭m6/9

Ab minor

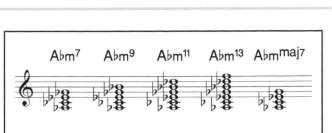

Abm⁷

Abm⁹

Abm¹¹

Abm¹³

Ab

Abm^maj7

See also: Abm⁷♭⁵ *(or Ab∅)*

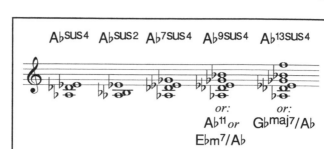

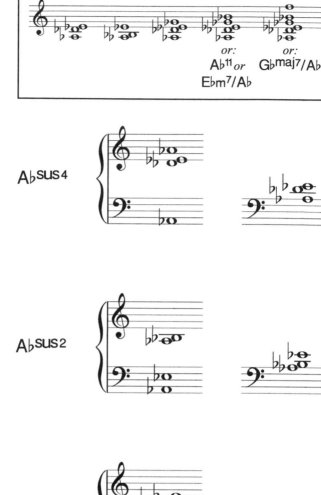

A♭

See also: A♭7sus4♭9, A♭13sus4♭9, G♭/A♭, E♭m7/A♭, G♭maj7/A♭

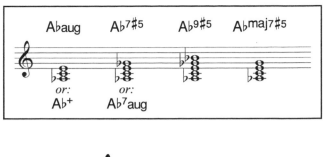

Abaug

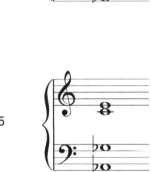

Ab7#5

Ab7#5

Ab9#5

Ab

Abmaj7#5

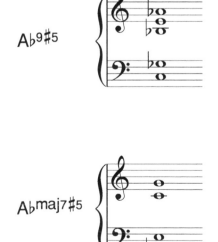

See also: Ab7b9b13, Ab7#9b13

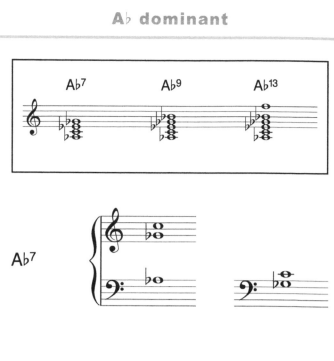

A♭7

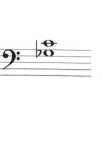

A♭9

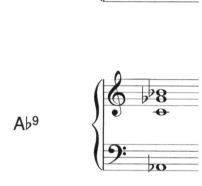

A♭9

A♭13

A♭13

See also: A♭7sus4, A♭7♭5, A♭7♯5, A♭7♭9, A♭7♯9, A♭7sus4♭9, A♭7♭9♭13, A♭7♯9♭13, A♭9♯11, A♭13♭9♯11, G♭/A♭, E♭m7/A♭, G♭maj7/A♭, D/A♭, F/A♭ (and any extended variants of these chords)

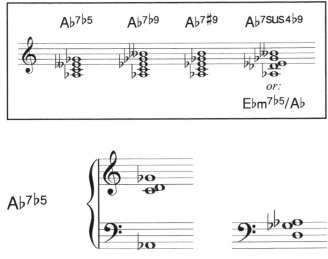

A♭⁷♭⁵

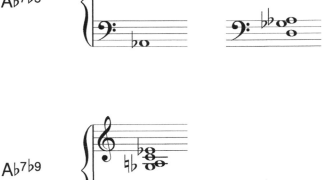

A♭⁷♭⁹

A♭⁷♭⁹

A♭⁷♯⁹

A♭

A♭⁷sus4♭⁹

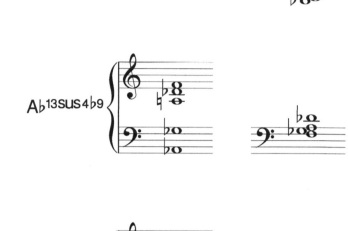

A♭13♭9

A♭13sus4♭9

A♭7♭9♭13

A♭7♯9♭13

See also: F/A♭

A♭9♯11   A♭13♯11   A♭13♭9♯11

A♭9♯11

A♭9♯11

A♭13♯11

A♭13♯11

A♭

A♭13♭9♯11
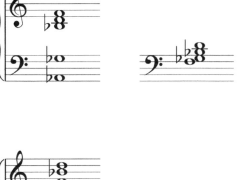

See also: D/A♭

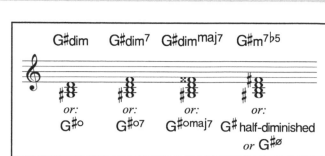

A♭

G♭/A♭
or:
A♭¹¹
or
A♭⁹sus4

E♭m⁷/A♭
or:
A♭¹¹
or
A♭⁹sus4

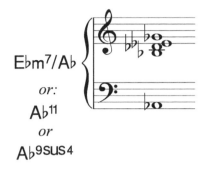

G♭maj7/A♭
or:
A♭¹³sus4

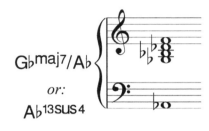

D/A♭
or:
A♭⁷♭9♯11
or
A♭⁷♭5♭9

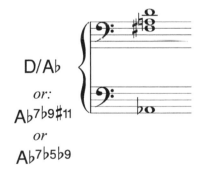

A♭

F/A♭
or:
A♭¹³♭9

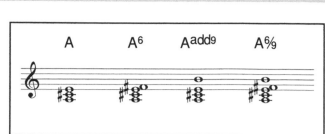

A A⁶ Aadd9 A⁶⁄₉

A⁶

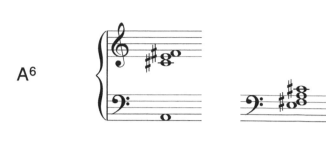

A⁶

Aadd9

A⁶⁄₉

A⁶⁄₉

A

A major

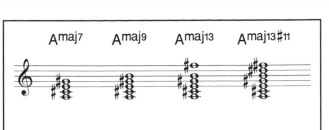

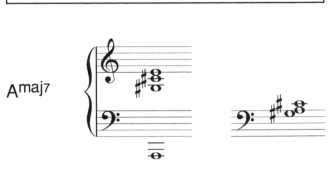
Amaj7

Amaj9

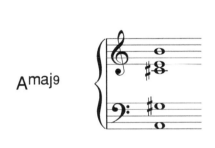
Amaj9

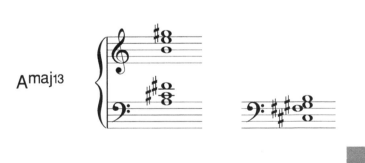
Amaj13

A

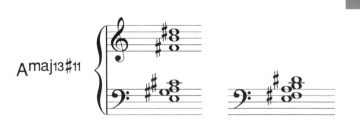
Amaj13♯11

See also: A^maj7♯5

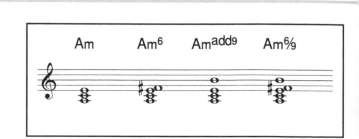

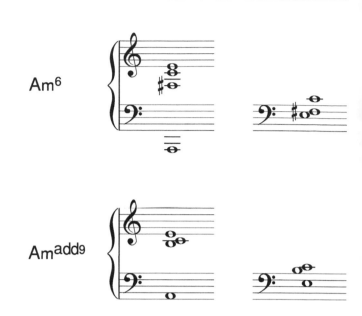

Am⁶

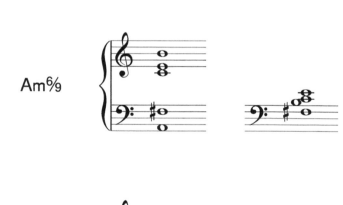

Am^add9

Am⁶⁄₉

Am⁶⁄₉

A

Am⁶⁄₉

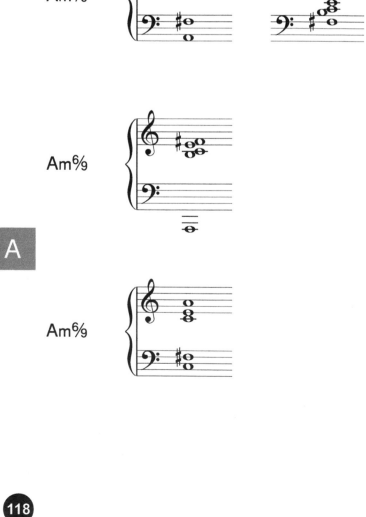

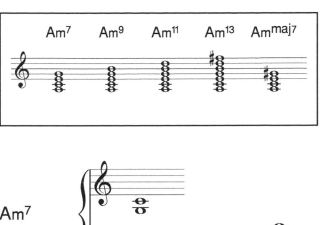

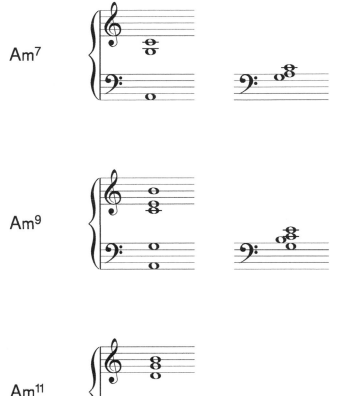

A

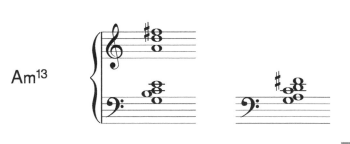

See also: Am$^{7\flat5}$ *(or A$^\emptyset$)*

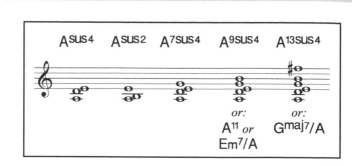

A^{SUS4}

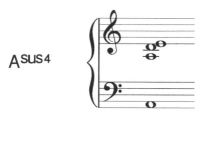

A^{SUS2}

A^{7SUS4}

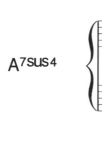

A^{9SUS4}

A^{13SUS4}

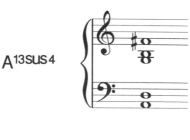

A

See also: $A^{7SUS4\flat9}$, $A^{13SUS4\flat9}$, G/A, Em^7/A, G^{maj7}/A

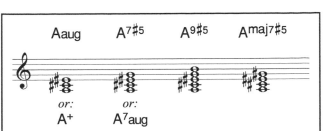

or: A⁺   *or:* A⁷aug

Aaug

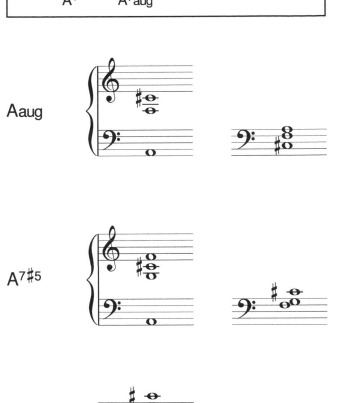

A⁷♯5

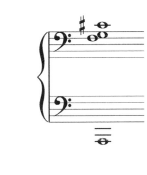

A⁷♯5

A⁹♯5

A

Amaj7♯5

See also: A⁷♭9♭13, A⁷♯9♭13

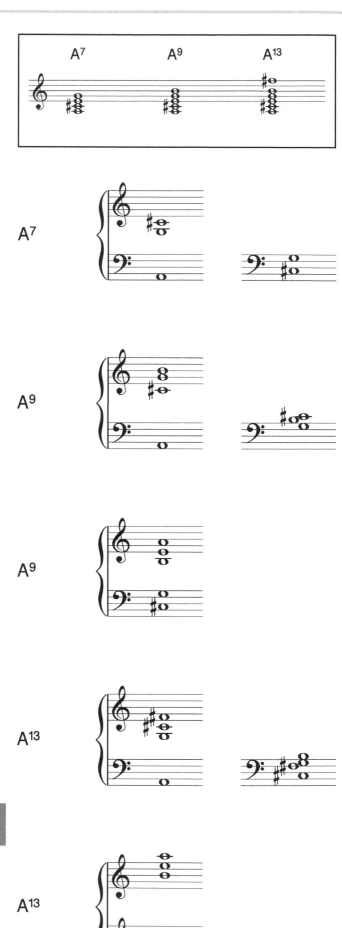

A⁷

A⁹

A⁹

A¹³

A¹³

See also: A⁷sus⁴, A⁷♭⁵, A⁷♯⁵, A⁷♭⁹, A⁷♯⁹, A⁷sus⁴♭⁹, A⁷♭⁹♭¹³, A⁷♯⁹♭¹³, A⁹♯¹¹, A¹³♭⁹♯¹¹, G/A, Em⁷/A, Gᵐᵃʲ⁷/A, E♭/A, F♯/A (and any extended variants of these chords)

A dominant

A⁷♭5

A⁷♭9

A⁷♭9

A⁷♯9

A

A⁷sus4♭9
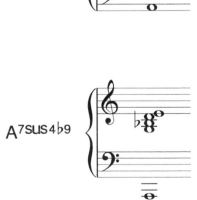

123

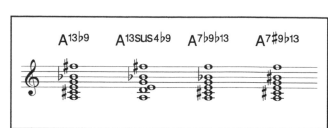

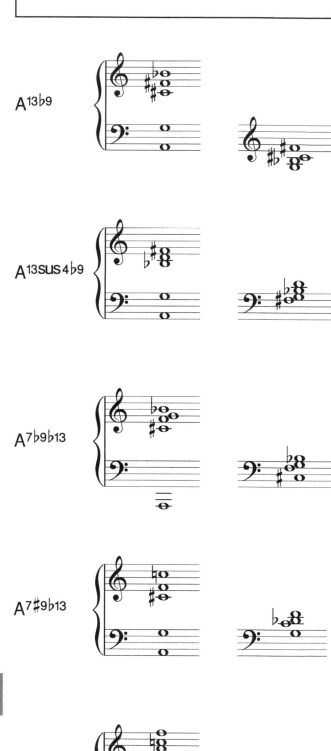

A^{13♭9}

A^{13sus4♭9}

A^{7♭9♭13}

A^{7♯9♭13}

A^{7♯9♭13}

A

See also: F♯/A

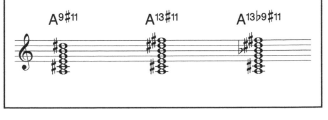

A⁹♯11

A⁹♯11

A¹³♯11

A¹³♯11

A¹³♭9♯11

See also: E♭/A

A

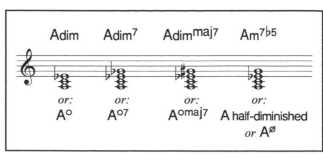

Adim — or: A°
Adim⁷ — or: A°⁷
Adim^maj7 — or: A°maj7
Am^7♭5 — or: A half-diminished or A^ø

Adim

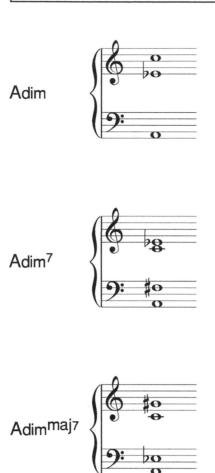

Adim⁷

Adim^maj7

Am^7♭5

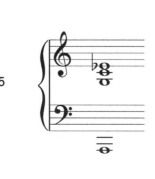

Am^7♭5

G/A
or:
A^{11}
or
A^{9}sus^{4}

Em^{7}/A
or:
A^{11}
or
A^{9}sus^{4}

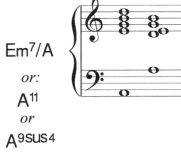

G^{maj7}/A
or:
A^{13}sus^{4}

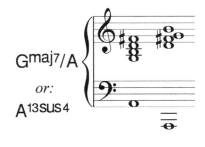

E♭/A
or:
A$^{7♭9♯11}$
or
A$^{7♭5♭9}$

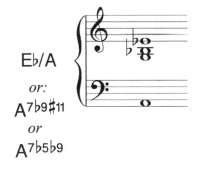

F♯/A
or:
A$^{13♭9}$

A

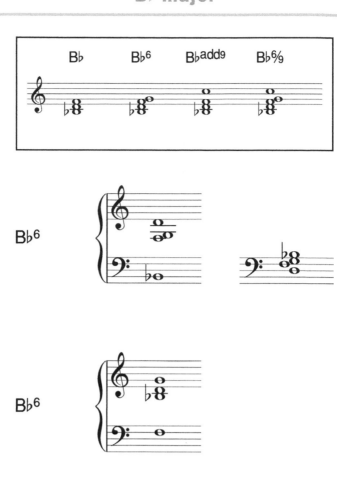

B♭   B♭6   B♭add9   B♭6/9

B♭6

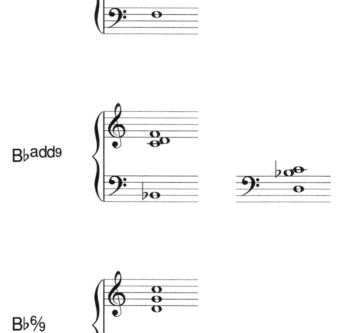

B♭6

B♭add9

B♭6/9

B♭

B♭6/9

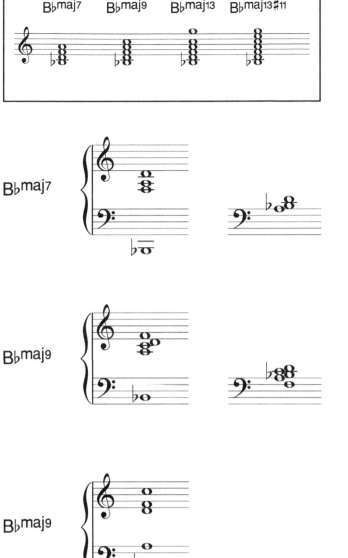

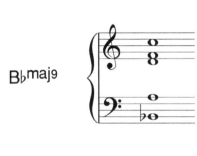

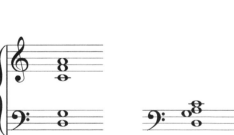

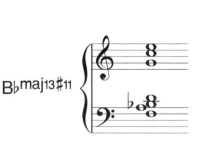

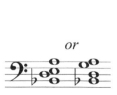

B♭

See also: B♭maj7♯5

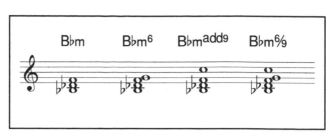

B♭m   B♭m⁶   B♭m^add9   B♭m⁶/₉

B♭m⁶

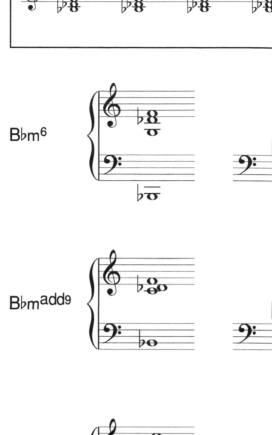

B♭m^add9

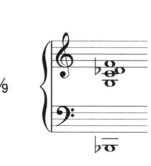

B♭m⁶/₉

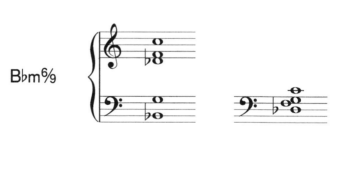

B♭m⁶/₉

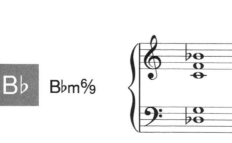

B♭m⁶/₉

B♭

Bb minor

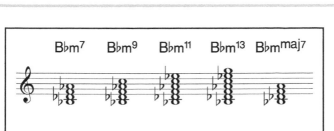

Bbm⁷

Bbm⁹

Bbm¹¹

Bbm¹³

Bbmᵐᵃʲ⁷

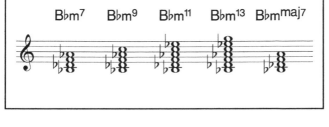

Bb

See also: Bbm⁷♭⁵ *(or Bb∅)*

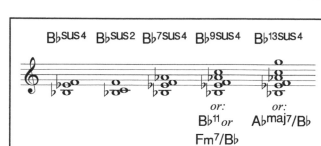

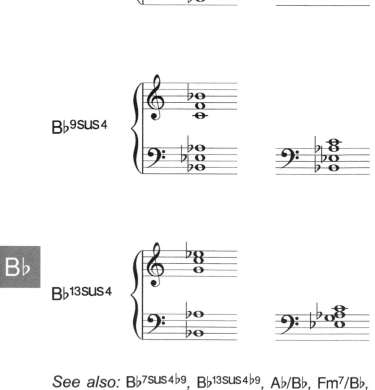

B♭sus4

B♭sus2

B♭7sus4

B♭9sus4

B♭

B♭13sus4

See also: B♭7sus4♭9, B♭13sus4♭9, A♭/B♭, Fm7/B♭, A♭maj7/B♭

Bb augmented

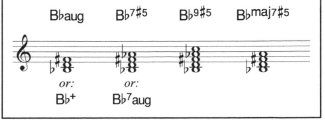

Bbaug

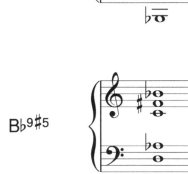

Bb7#5

Bb7#5

Bb9#5

Bbmaj7#5

See also: Bb7b9b13, Bb7#9b13

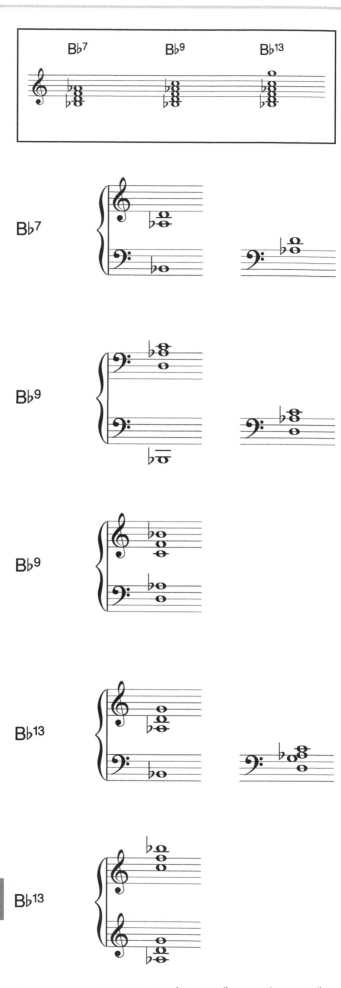

See also: B♭⁷ˢᵘˢ⁴, B♭⁷♭⁵, B♭⁷♯⁵, B♭⁷♭⁹, B♭⁷♯⁹, B♭⁷ˢᵘˢ⁴♭⁹, B♭⁷♭⁹♭¹³, B♭⁷♯⁹♭¹³, B♭⁹♯¹¹, B♭¹³♭⁹♯¹¹, A♭/B♭, Fm⁷/B♭, A♭ᵐᵃʲ⁷/B♭, E/B♭, G/B♭ (and any extended variants of these chords)

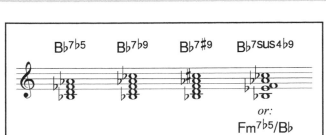

or:
Fm⁷♭⁵/B♭

B♭⁷♭⁵

B♭⁷♭⁹

B♭⁷♭⁹

B♭⁷♯⁹

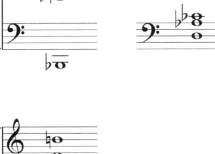

B♭⁷ˢᵘˢ⁴♭⁹

B♭

Bb13b9

Bb13sus4b9

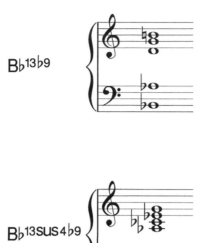

Bb7b9b13

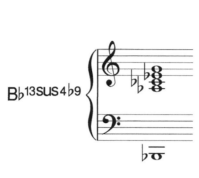

Bb7#9b13

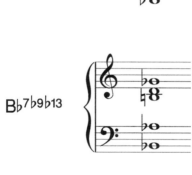

Bb7#9b13

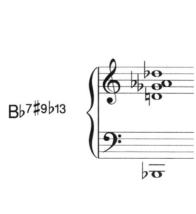

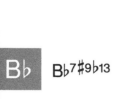

Bb

See also: G/B♭

B♭ dominant

B♭9♯11

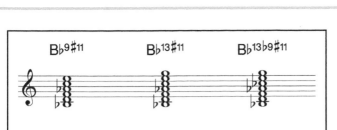

B♭9♯11

B♭13♯11

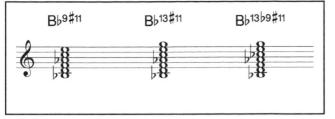

B♭13♯11

B♭13♭9♯11

Bb

See also: E/B♭

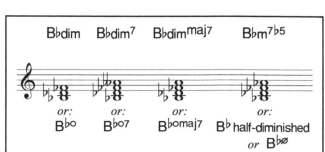

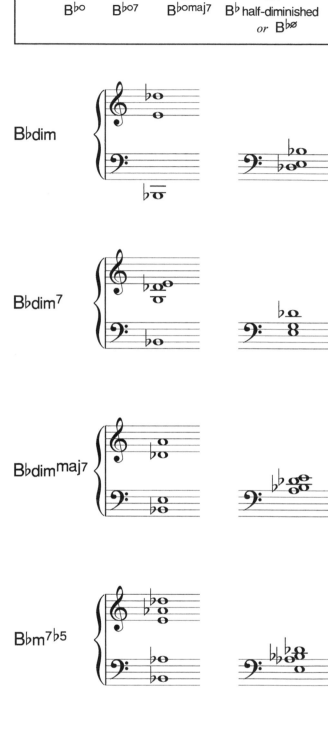

B♭dim

B♭dim⁷

B♭dim^maj7

B♭m⁷♭⁵

B♭m⁷♭⁵

A♭/B♭
or:
B♭11
or
B♭9sus4

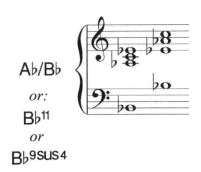

Fm7/B♭
or:
B♭11
or
B♭9sus4

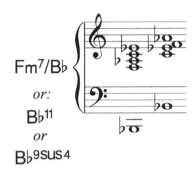

A♭maj7/B♭
or:
B♭13sus4

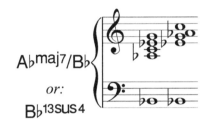

E/B♭
or:
B♭7♭9♯11
or
B♭7♭5♭9

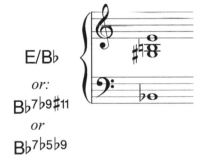

G/B♭
or:
B♭13♭9

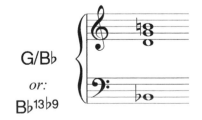

B♭

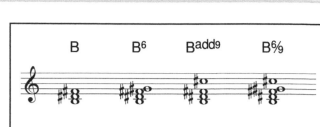

B⁶

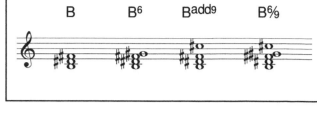

B⁶

Badd9

B6⁄9

B6⁄9

B

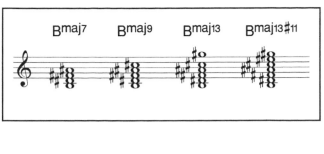

Bmaj7

Bmaj9

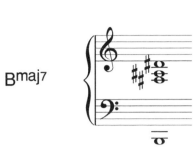

Bmaj9

Bmaj13

Bmaj13#11

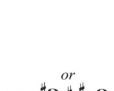

or

B

See also: Bmaj7#5

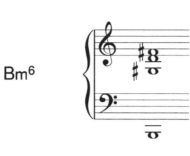

Bm⁶

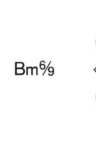

Bmadd9

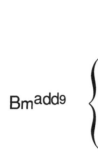

Bm⁶/9

Bm⁶/9

Bm⁶/9

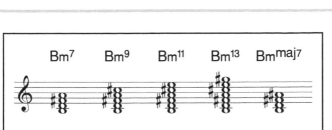

Bm⁷

Bm⁹

Bm¹¹

Bm¹³

Bmᵐᵃʲ⁷

See also: Bm⁷♭⁵ *(or* B∅*)*

B

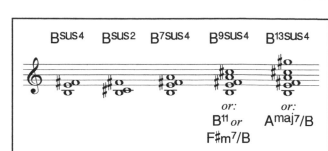

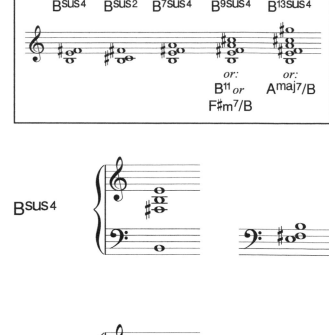

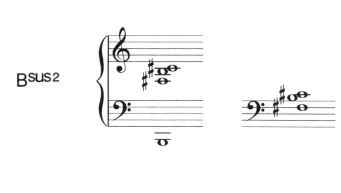

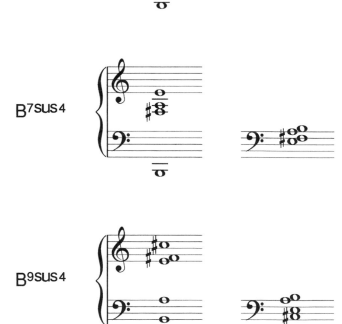

See also: B⁷ˢᵘˢ⁴♭⁹, B¹³ˢᵘˢ⁴♭⁹, A/B, F♯m⁷/B, Aᵐᵃʲ⁷/B

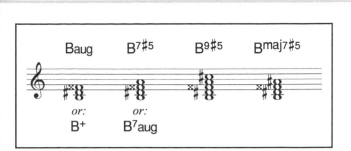

Baug

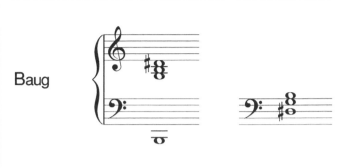

B⁷♯5

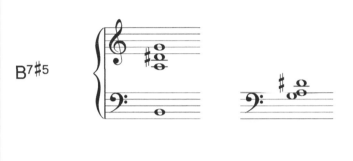

B⁷♯5

B⁹♯5

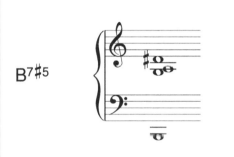

Bmaj7♯5

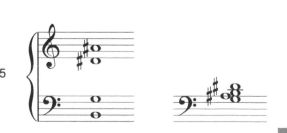

See also: B⁷♭9♭13, B⁷♯9♭13

B

See also: B⁷ˢᵘˢ⁴, B⁷ᵇ⁵, B⁷♯⁵, B⁷ᵇ⁹, B⁷♯⁹, B⁷ˢᵘˢ⁴ᵇ⁹, B⁷ᵇ⁹ᵇ¹³, B⁷♯⁹ᵇ¹³, B⁹♯¹¹, B¹³ᵇ⁹♯¹¹, A/B, F♯m⁷/B, Aᵐᵃʲ⁷/B, F/B, G♯/B (and any extended variants of these chords)

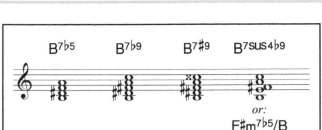

B⁷♭⁵ B⁷♭⁹ B⁷♯⁹ B⁷sus4♭⁹

or:
F♯m⁷♭⁵/B

B⁷♭⁵
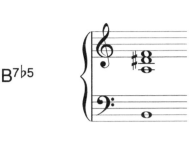

B⁷♭⁹

B⁷♭⁹

B⁷♯⁹

B⁷sus4♭⁹

B

B dominant

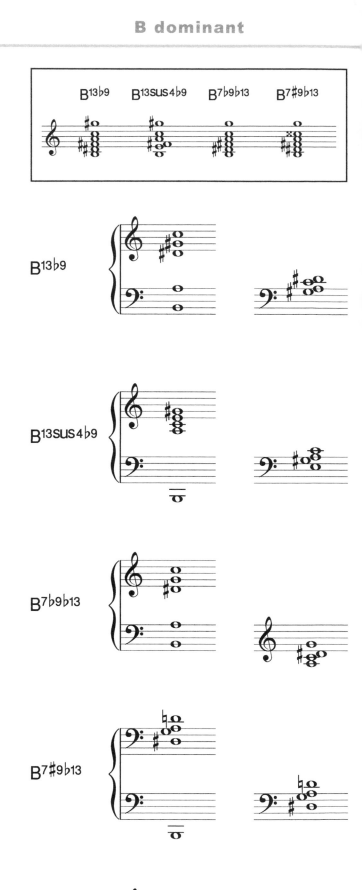

See also: G♯/B

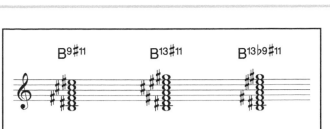

$B^{9\sharp11}$

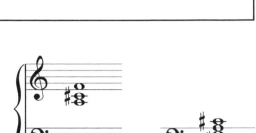

$B^{9\sharp11}$

$B^{13\sharp11}$

$B^{13\sharp11}$

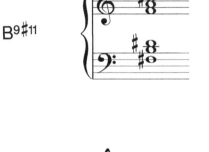

$B^{13\flat9\sharp11}$

See also: F/B

B

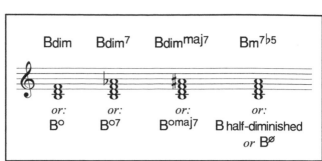

Bdim   Bdim⁷   Bdim^maj7   Bm⁷♭⁵

or: *or:*   *or:*   *or:*

B°   B°⁷   B°maj7   B half-diminished

or B⌀

Bdim

Bdim⁷

Bdim^maj7

Bm⁷♭⁵

Bm⁷♭⁵

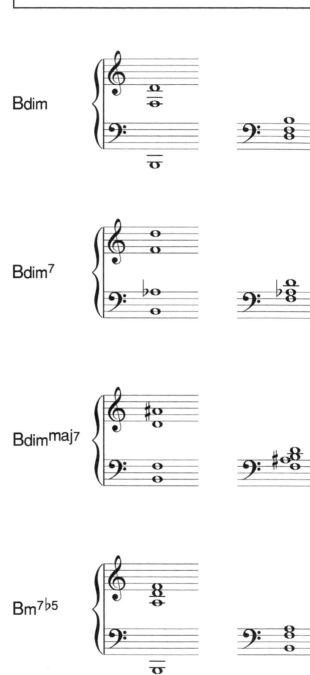

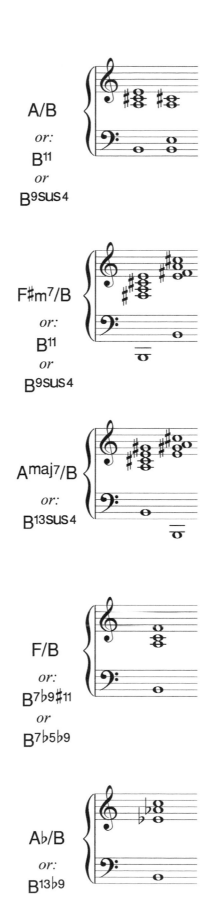

A/B
or:
B^{11}
or
B^{9}sus4

F#m^{7}/B
or:
B^{11}
or
B^{9}sus4

A^{maj7}/B
or:
B^{13}sus4

F/B
or:
B$^{7b9\sharp11}$
or
B^{7b5b9}

Ab/B
or:
B^{13b9}

Bringing you the words and the music

- Book-and-CD titles with high quality backing tracks for you to play along to. Now you can play guitar or piano with your favourite artist... or simply sing along!

- Audition songbooks with CD backing tracks for both male and female singers for all those with stars in their eyes.

- Can't read music? No problem, you can still play all the hits with our wide range of chord songbooks.

- Check out our range of instrumental tutorial titles, taking you from novice to expert in no time at all!

- Musical how scores include *The Phantom Of The Opera*, *Les Misérables*, *Mamma Mia* and many more hit productions.

- DVD master classes featuring the techniques of top artists.